Collins Mapstart²

Professor Simon Catling
Research Leader, Department of Early Childhood and Primary
Oxford Brookes University

CW00865562

contents

looking down at everyday objects

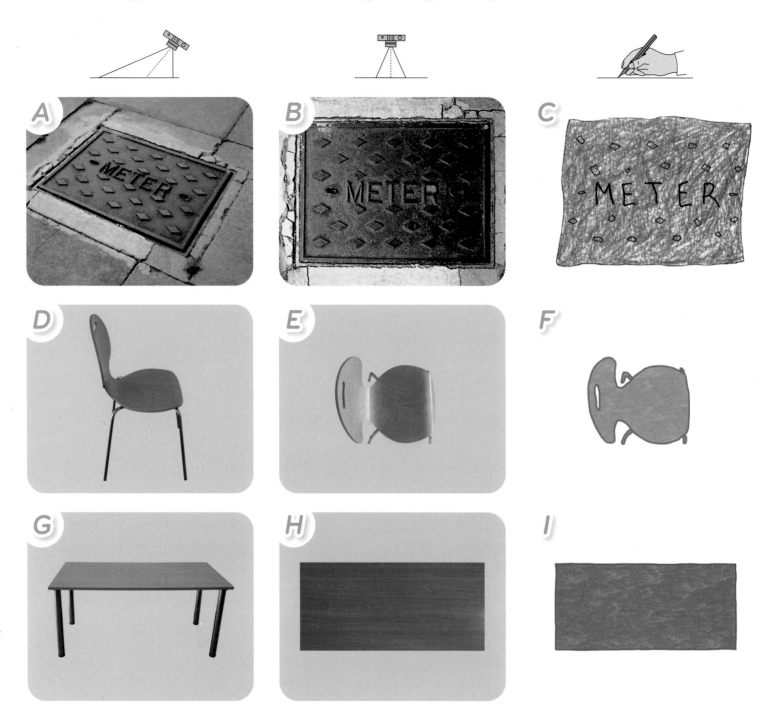

Photos **A**, **D** and **G** show objects you can see every day. The photos were taken **looking down from the side**.

Photos **B**, **E** and **H** were taken **looking down from straight above**. You can see the shape of each object from above.

C, **F** and **I** are **plans** of each object. They show the **shape** of each object looking down from straight above.

1 Name the objects in A, D and G.

2 What does a plan show?

3 Draw a plan of an object on your table.

J

K

L

M

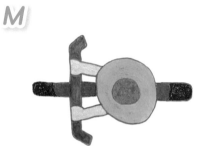

lamp   helicopter

jug   person on
         a bike

truck

         shoe

banana   book

N

O

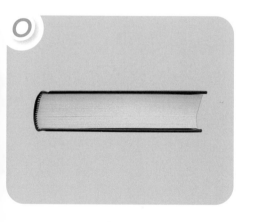

P

Q

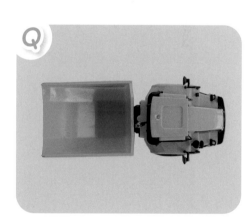

Look at the photos and plans on this page.
They show the **view** looking straight down
from above.
The names of each object are in the box.
Match the name with the object.

1   Name the object in each photo.
2   Name the object in each plan.
3   Draw a plan of the object in each photo.
4   Draw plans of some objects in your
    classroom.

A

B

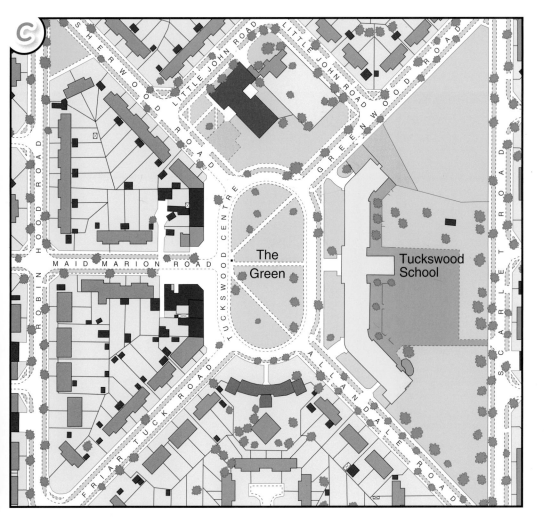

KEY

These shapes and colours show

 Houses

 Flats

 Garages and Sheds

 Glasshouses

Shops

Post Office

 Gardens, Walls and Fences

Paddling pool

 Trees

Road and Pavement

Path

· Phone box

These colours show

School

Church

Playground

Car park

Grass

A and B are photos of Tuckswood School. They were taken from a plane.

A is an **oblique view** of the school. You are looking down at the back of the school. You can see the school building and the playground. You can see some of the area around the school. At the front of the school you can see The Green and the shops.

In photo B you are looking straight down at the school. This is called a **vertical view**. In the vertical view you can see the shape of the school and some of the roads and buildings near the school.

C is a map of Tuckswood School. It shows the same area you can see in photo B. Use the **key** to see what the shapes and colours show. The roads are named on the map.

1 Which colour on the map shows the school building?

2 How many roads are named on map C?

3 Which other places are named on the map?

4 Which buildings are the car parks next to?

5 What would you walk across to go from the Post Office to the school?

6 Why do you think the road around The Green is called Tuckswood Centre?

satellite photo of the British Isles

A is a satellite photo of the British Isles. It shows the shape of the British Isles. There are many islands in the British Isles. The two largest islands are named in the photo.

B is a map of the British Isles. It shows the countries in the British Isles. The four countries coloured yellow make up the United Kingdom.

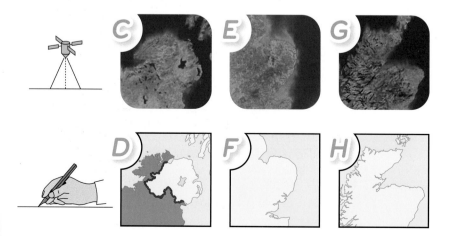

1 Which are the two largest islands in the British Isles?

2 Name the four countries that are part of the United Kingdom.

3 Which part of Ireland is part of the United Kingdom?

4 Look at the area in photo C and map D.
Look at its shape. Find it in A. Is it in Ireland or Britain?

5 Look at the area in photo E and map F. Look at its shape. Find it in B. Which country is it in?

6 Which country is the area in G and H in?

7 In which country of the British Isles do you live?

satellite photo of Europe

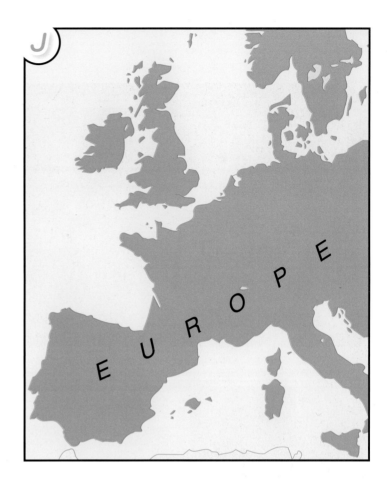

E U R O P E

I is another photo taken by a satellite. It shows a part of the Earth named Europe. Find Ireland and Britain on the photo. They look small in this photo.

J is a map of the part of Europe you can see in I. It shows the land and sea. Ireland and Britain are part of Europe. There are many other islands that are part of Europe. Find them in I and J.

1 What colour is the sea in I and K?

2 Which colour shows the land in J?

3 Draw the shape of the largest island in Europe.

4 Draw the shape of two more islands you can see in Europe.

5 Find Europe in K. Name another large area of land you can see.

6 Look at a globe and find out which parts of the Earth you cannot see in K.

K is another photo taken from space. It shows a view of the Earth. Through the clouds you can see the land and sea.

K

Europe

Asia

Africa

satellite photo of the Earth

what is a plan?

A is a photo of a classroom. You can see most of the room, but not all of it. Look at **B**. It shows how the classroom would look if you could take a photo looking down from straight above. It is a **vertical view** of the classroom.

Find **where** some of the things you can see in photo **A** are in view **B**. Find some objects in **B** that you cannot see in photo **A**.

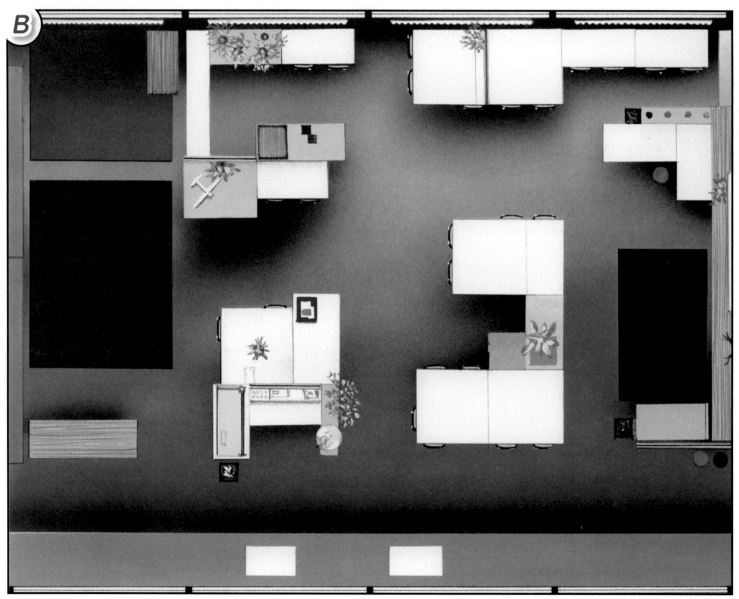

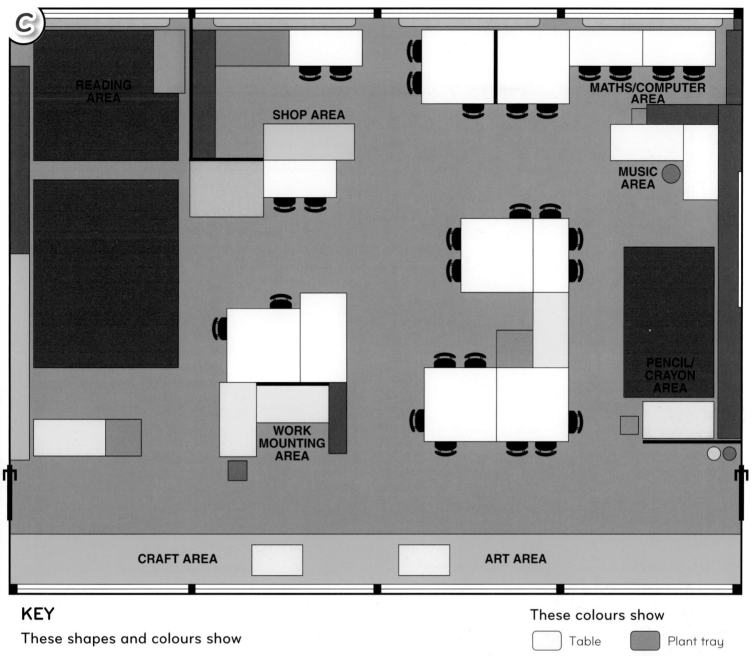

KEY

These shapes and colours show

▮ Stand	▬ Door	▭ Whiteboard	▭ Sink
▮ Shelves	⌒ Seat	▭ Radiator	▮◦ Bin and Tub
▬ Screen	● Stool	▭ Window	▮ Box

These colours show

▭ Table	▮ Plant tray
▭ Trolley	▮ Cupboards
▮ Drawer unit	▮ Floor
▮ Shop unit	▮ Carpet

C is a plan of the classroom. It shows the **layout** of the room. You can see where things are. It also shows the shapes of the furniture in the room.

The **key** tells you **what** the shapes and colours mean on the plan.

Some areas in the room have been named.

1 How many seats does plan **C** show?

2 Which colour in the key shows carpets?

3 Name three objects next to the largest carpet.

4 Name three objects you pass on your right going from the shop to the smallest carpet.

9

looking at plans – a school

A

Look at photos **A** and **B**. They were taken from a plane. They show part of St. Alban's School.

A is an **oblique view** looking down at the front of the main school building.

B is a **vertical view** looking straight down on the same building.

In **B** you can see the shape of the building on the ground.

1 Does the school have a car park? What is your evidence?

2 Draw or trace the shape of the school building. Colour it in. Draw round it the paths you can see.

3 How many corners has the shape of the school building?

B

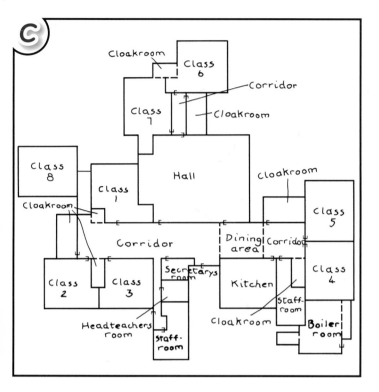

Photos **A** and **B** show you the outside of St. Alban's School.

C is a plan of the inside of the school. It shows where the rooms are in the school.

Plan **C** was used to make a **survey** of the rooms. It is a **base plan**. It shows only the rooms.

The survey was about what the rooms in the main school building are used for. What each room is used for was written on the base plan.

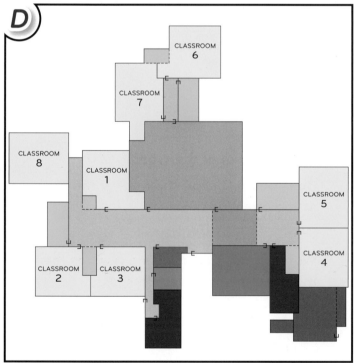

Plan **D** was made after the survey. It has been coloured in to show what each of the rooms is used for.

Some of the rooms have been numbered. Use the **key** to help you see what each colour shows.

1 How were the classrooms shown on the base plan?

2 Which colour shows the hall on plan **D**?

3 What does yellow show on plan **D**?

4 Which rooms are next to the headteacher's room?

5 How many rooms are next to the hall?

6 Which two rooms are furthest apart in the main building?

7 Which rooms do you pass on your right going from classroom 2 to classroom 4?

8 Why do you think the classrooms are numbered on the plans?

KEY

Cloakroom

Dining area

Kitchen

Classroom

Secretary's room

Headteacher's room

Staffroom

Hall

Boiler room

Corridor

← Door

11

looking at plans – school grounds

A

B

C

D

Photo **A** shows the buildings, playground and playing field of St. Alban's School. It is an oblique view of the school.

Photos **B**, **C** and **D** were taken on the ground.

Photo **B** shows the way into the school.

Look carefully at **C** and **D** to see which parts of the school they show.

Photo **E** is a vertical view of the school grounds.

The parts of the school have been named. Find them on photo **A**.

F is a plan of the school grounds. It was made after a survey of the use of the school grounds. Colours have been used to show the different parts of the school. The key shows what the colours mean. The plan also shows the rooms inside the school buildings.

1 Which photo was taken looking straight down at the school?

2 Does photo **C** show the front or the back of the main building?

3 What can you see in photo **D**?

4 Was photo **D** taken looking towards the main building or away from it?

5 Which parts of the school are named in photo **E**?

6 Which colour shows the playing field in plan **F**?

7 Find the car park. Is it at the front or the back of the school?

8 Use plan **F** to help you. Which classrooms can you see in photo **C**?

E

Playground

Playing field

Climbing frame

Main building

Car park

Pre-school

F

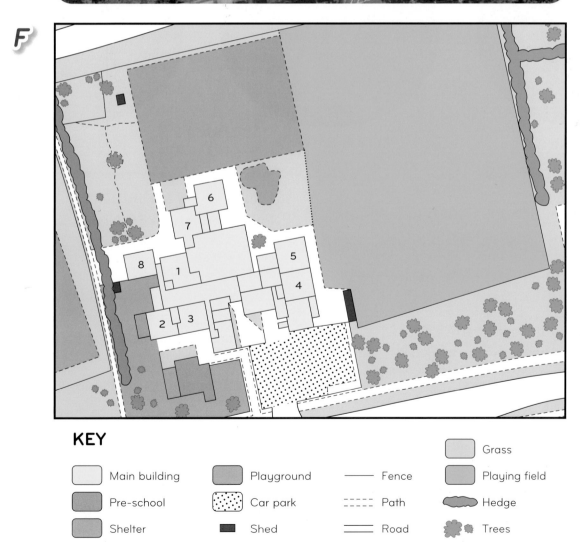

| 6 |
| 7 |
| 8 | 1 |
| 5 |
| 4 |
| 2 | 3 |

KEY

▢ Main building	▢ Playground	—— Fence	▢ Grass
▢ Pre-school	▢ Car park	- - - Path	▢ Playing field
▢ Shelter	▢ Shed	═══ Road	🌳 Hedge
			🌲 Trees

maps of a local area – the school locality

church

block of flats

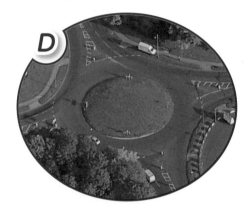

roundabout

Photo **A** is an oblique view of the area around St. Alban's School. Find it in the photo. It shows part of the local area of the school.

Photos **B**, **C** and **D** show three features you can see in **A**.

Photo **F** is a vertical view of the area. **G** is a **map** of the area in photo **F**. The different parts of the local area have been named on the map. Find St. Alban's School on **A**, **F** and **G**.

E

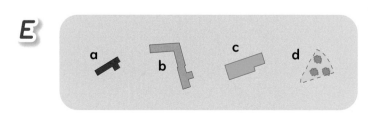

1 Look at photo **B**. Find it in **A**. Is it to the left or right of St. Alban's School?

2 What is the name of the school next to St. Alban's School?

3 Look at photo **C**. Find the block of flats in **A**. Draw the shape of the flats that you would see looking straight down from above.

4 What does grey show on map **G**?

5 Name two roads going into the feature in **D**.

6 In box **E** you can see four features from map **G**. Say what they are and which part of the local area they are in.

7 If you walked from the roundabout towards Monkswick Road, what would you pass on your right?

F

G

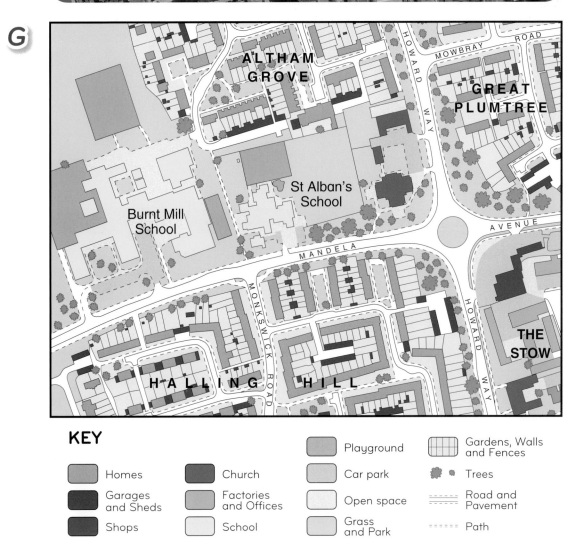

ALTHAM GROVE

MOWBRAY ROAD

HOWARD WAY

GREAT PLUMTREE

St Alban's School

Burnt Mill School

AVENUE

MANDELA

MONKSWICK ROAD

HOWARD WAY

THE STOW

HALLING HILL

KEY

Homes	Church	Playground	Gardens, Walls and Fences
Garages and Sheds	Factories and Offices	Car park	Trees
Shops	School	Open space	Road and Pavement
		Grass and Park	Path

making a map

From time to time new people move into the flats near Emma's home in Simon's Close. They need to know where the local shops are in the village of Wheatley. Emma wanted to make a map to show them the way to the shops from the flats.

First Emma drew map **A**.
She drew it from memory, putting in the shops she remembered that are near to the flats.
One shop near the flats is the Co-op shop in photo **B**.

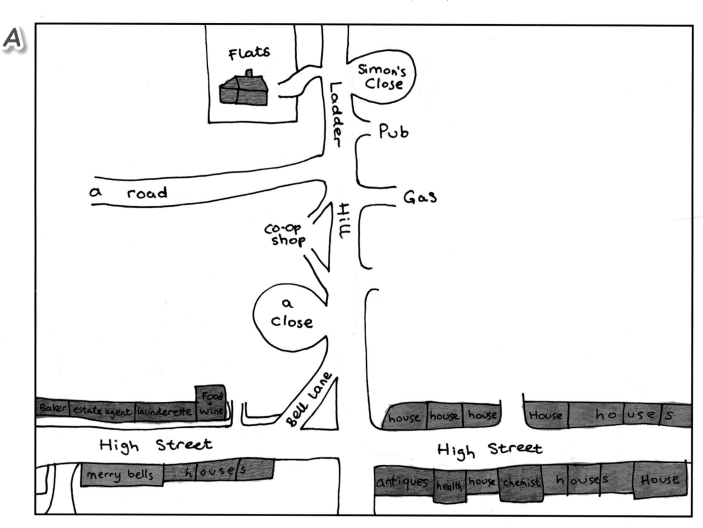

A

Flats
Simon's Close
Ladder
Pub
a road
Gas
Co-op shop
Hill
a close
Bell Lane
Baker | estate agent | launderette | Food + Wine
house | house | house
House | houses
High Street
merry bells | houses
High Street
antiques | health | house | chemist | houses | House

B

1 Find the flats on map **A**. Which road are the flats next to?

2 Along which road are most shops?

3 What other places did Emma draw beside the shops?

4 Why would it help someone in the flats to know where the chemist is?

5 How many shops does Emma show on map **A**?

When she had finished her map Emma wanted to be sure the map showed all the shops and the route to them. She went out with her map to check that it was accurate.

She found that she had to change some of the places she had drawn so that her map was correct. Then she drew map **C** to show the shops and roads more accurately.

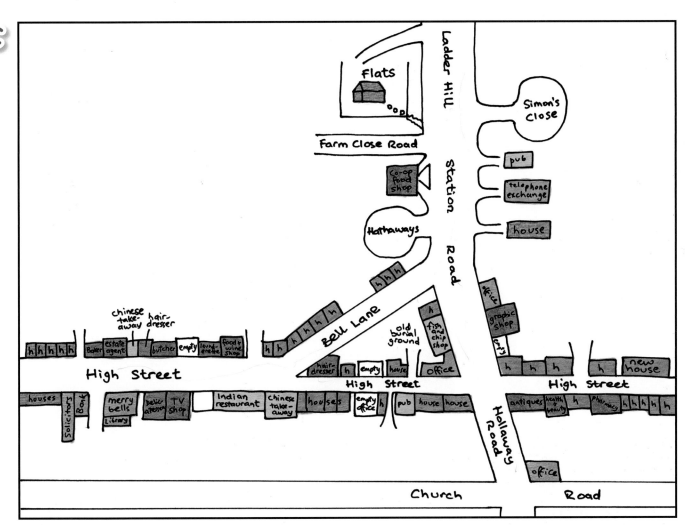

1 Name five shops on map **C** which are not on map **A**.

2 Which roads would you walk along to go from the flats to the baker?

3 List some other changes Emma made to her map when she redrew it.

4 Draw a map to show the way to a place near your home, so that someone else can use it to get there.

story maps

In the story of **Fantastic Mr. Fox** there are three farmers from whom Mr. Fox is always stealing food. The farmers are Farmer Boggis, Farmer Bunce and Farmer Bean.

In **A** you can see the three farms. Farmer Bean lives in a farm which has trees around it. Find it. Farmer Boggis lives opposite Farmer Bean. Farmer Bunce lives in the farm close by the stream.

A

Mr. Fox steals chickens from Farmer Boggis. He takes ducks and geese from Farmer Bunce and he steals turkeys from Farmer Bean.

1 Which farm is highest up the side of the valley?

2 Whose farm is in the bottom of the valley?

3 Whose farm is by the large tree on the cliff?

4 Which two farms are on the same side of the stream?

5 Whose farm has an orchard of apple trees?

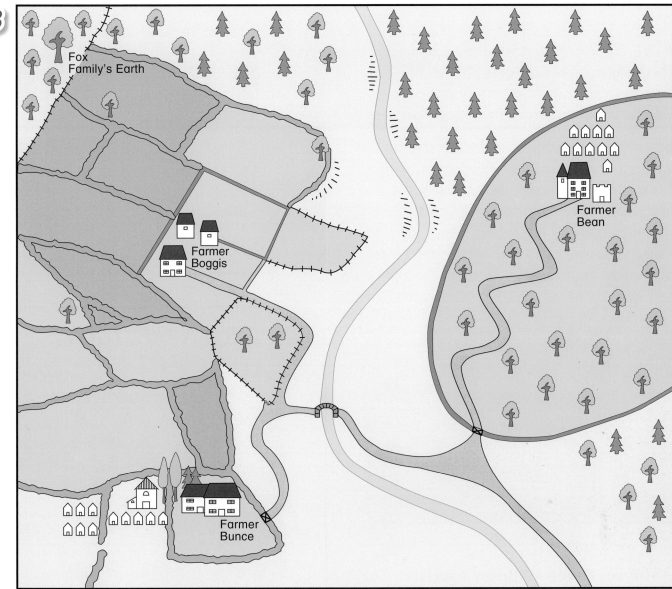

B is a picture map of the area where farmers Bean, Boggis and Bunce live. You can also see where the Fox family live in their earth.

Map **B** shows where the farmers keep their turkeys, chickens, ducks and geese. It shows the fields around the farms. Some of the fields are for grazing and some are ploughed for planting crops like wheat and barley.

1 Which farmer does Mr. Fox live nearest to?

2 Which colour shows fields animals can graze in? Use picture **A** to help you.

3 Find Farmer Bean's turkey houses on map **B**. Are they in front of or behind his farm house?

4 Why can you not see Farmer Bean's turkey houses in picture **A**?

5 Make a key for the map to show what the pictures and colours mean.

19

all sorts of maps

There are all sorts of maps you can find.
You see maps on road signs.
You find them in newspapers and adverts.
You can buy postcards with maps on them.

Maps can tell you lots of different things.
Some maps help you see which way to go,
like the road sign map in **A**. Maps can be
used to show where places are, like the
advert map in **C**. Newspapers use maps to
show where something has happened, like
in car break-ins in **D**.

A

B

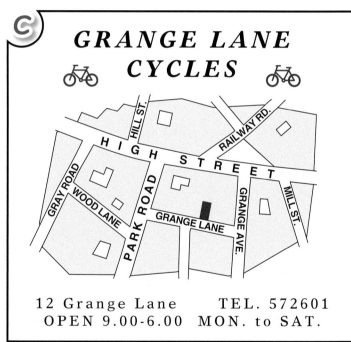

C

**GRANGE LANE
CYCLES**

12 Grange Lane   TEL. 572601
OPEN 9.00-6.00   MON. to SAT.

D

Thieves fleece Windsor tourists

Foreign visitors to the royal town of Windsor have become an easy target for thieves operating in the area. In the past ten weeks alone, valuables worth £150,000 have been stolen from foreign nationals. American tourists are the thieves' main victims but visitors from Canada, Germany and other European countries have also been targeted.

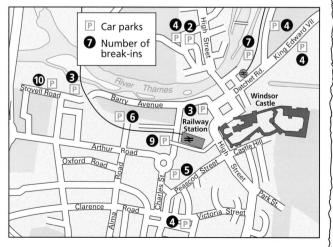

1 Which map would help someone driving a car?

2 Map **B** shows a shopping centre. What would be named on a shopping centre map?

3 Why would an advert like **C** include a map?

4 You see map **A** from your car. Would you turn left or right at the roundabout to go to Dingwall?

5 Use map **D** to write a report for the newspaper about the car break-ins.

Maps can tell you about towns you can visit and about different places of interest to visit in a tourist area.

Postcard maps **E** and **F** are often bought and sent by tourists who visit York and the Yorkshire Dales. They show places of historic interest which are visited by tourists.

We can also look at maps on the internet and our mobile phones. **G** and **H** show two examples of maps. There are many types of maps you can find.

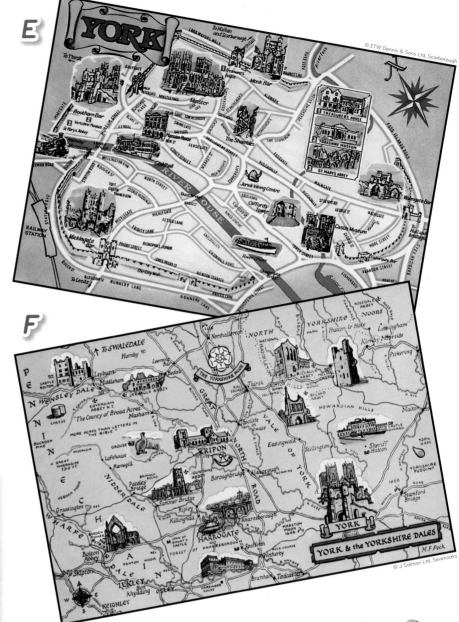

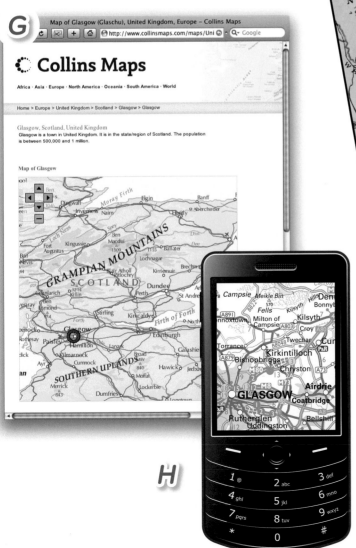

1 Look at map **E**. Name two places you could visit near the railway station.

2 Look at map **F**. Name two places you could visit to see castles.

3 Maps **E** and **F** have no key. Make a key for one of the postcard maps.

4 Why would you look for a map like that in **G**?

5 Why is it helpful to be able to use a map like **H** on your mobile phone?

6 Make a collection of all sorts of maps. See how many types of maps you can find. Obtain some of your maps using the internet.

north, east, south and west

A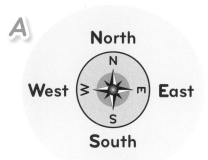

B is a **picture map** of a playground. Find the pond in the centre of the playground. Now find the slide.
To say which way it is from the pond to the slide, we can use **compass directions**.

The four points of the compass are **north**, **east**, **south** and **west**.
The **compass** in A shows that the slide is **north** of the pond. Find the letters N, E, S and W around the pond.

B

C

see-saw

D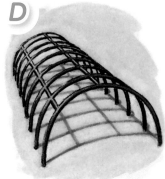

tunnel

1 Write what the letters N, E, S and W stand for.

2 What could you play on north of the pond?

3 Look at C. Which way is it from the pond?

4 Is D east or west of the pond?

5 Name the direction from the swings to the pond.

6 Make up a saying to help you remember the order of north, east, south and west using the first letters N, E, S and W.

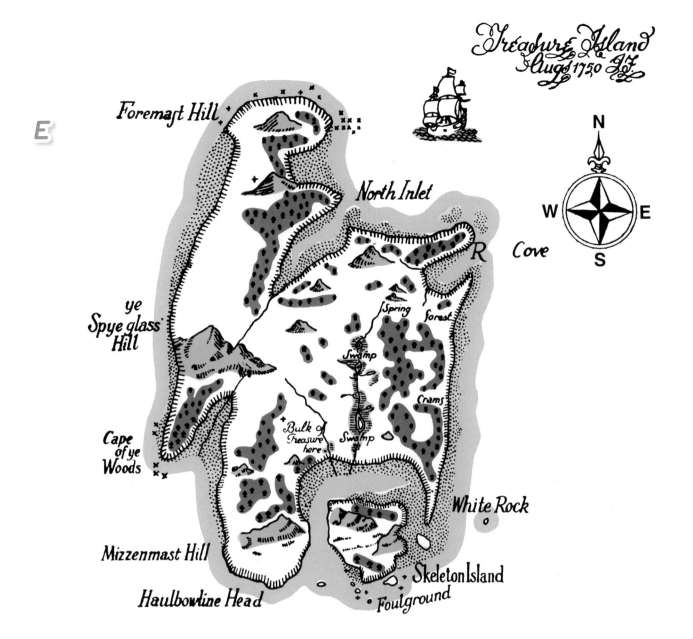

E

Treasure Island
Aug 1750 17

Foremast Hill

North Inlet

R Cove

ye Spye glass Hill

Spring forest

Swamp

Crams

Bulk of Treasure here

Swamp

Cape of ye Woods

White Rock

Mizzenmast Hill

Skeleton Island

Haulbowline Head Foulground

N W E S

Robert Louis Stevenson got the idea for his book, **Treasure Island**, when he drew a map of a treasure island. He thought it would make a good story. **E** is a map of the Treasure Island in his story. On his map of the island Robert Louis Stevenson included the **compass directions**, but he did not make a **key** for the map.
Look carefully at the map and work out what the shapes and colours show on the island.
He named some places on his island.
He marked where the treasure was hidden.

1 Make a key for the map.
2 Which place on the island is named after a compass direction?
3 Which way is Spye glass Hill from the swamp?
4 Name the hill in the north of the island.
5 Which direction is it from the swamp to the spring?
6 If you landed at the end of North Inlet, which way would you go to find the treasure?
7 Which parts of the island do not have sandy beaches?

directing the way

Look at the compass in **A**. It shows the four points of the compass. It also shows you four more compass directions, between north, east, south and west. Read what these are called.

We can use these directions to help find the way around the **picture map** of the park in **B**.

A

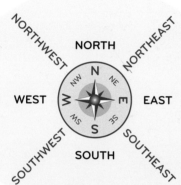

1 Which compass direction is it from North Gate to South Gate?

2 Is the lake in the northwest or the southwest of the park?

3 Which compass direction are the tennis courts from the fountain?

4 Follow these directions to find where to go:
You are in the playground. Go north and turn west towards the football pitch. Then turn northwest. Turn southwest at the next turning. Then turn north.
Which gate are you walking towards?

5 Say which way to go, using compass directions and turns, from the cafe to the toilets.

B

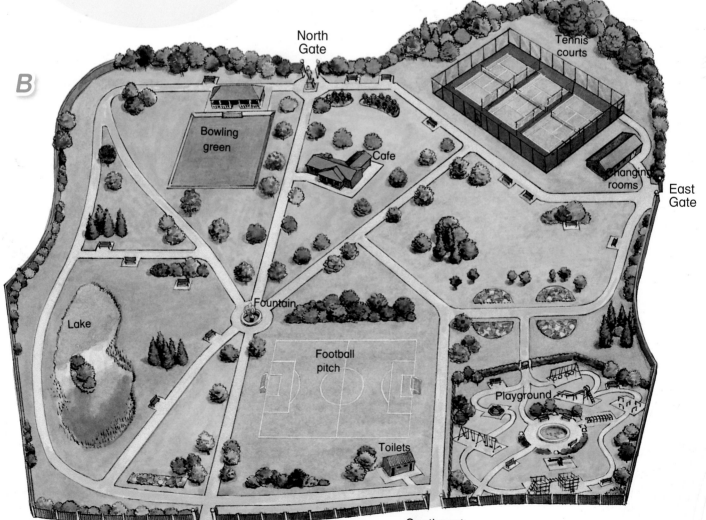

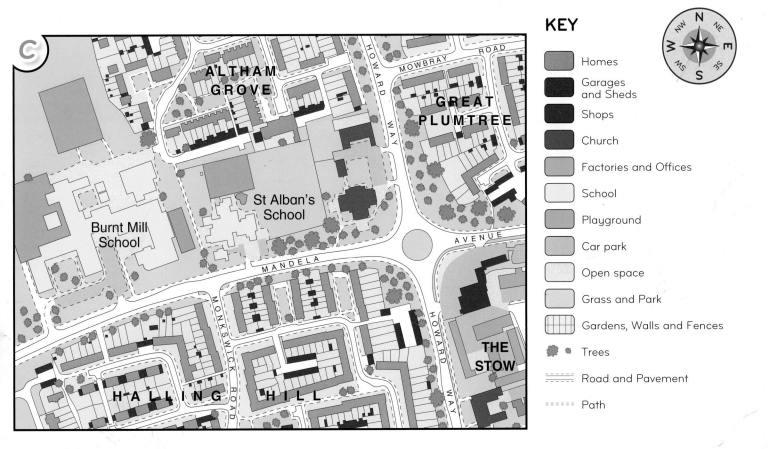

KEY

- Homes
- Garages and Sheds
- Shops
- Church
- Factories and Offices
- School
- Playground
- Car park
- Open space
- Grass and Park
- Gardens, Walls and Fences
- ✿ Trees
- ┈┈ Road and Pavement
- ┅┅ Path

Map **C** shows the area around St. Alban's School. It shows what the buildings near the school are used for. The roads are named on the map.

Four areas in the neighbourhood are named also. One is Altham Grove. It is north of the school.

1 Which school is southwest of Altham Grove?

2 Which area is southeast of St. Alban's School?

3 Does Mandela Avenue go north-south or east-west?

4 Which compass direction is it from Monkswick Road to The Stow?

5 Name the building northwest of the roundabout.

6 What is the name of the area southwest of Great Plumtree?

7 What are the buildings in the northeast of the area used for?

8 Find out where you have gone by following these instructions:
   Come out of St. Alban's School onto Mandela Avenue.
   Turn east.
   At the first road turn north.
   Go north.
   Turn east at the first road, then south at the next road.
Which area of the neighbourhood are you in? Name all of the roads you have walked along.

9 Make up some journeys of your own. Use compass directions to say which way to go.

25

locating places

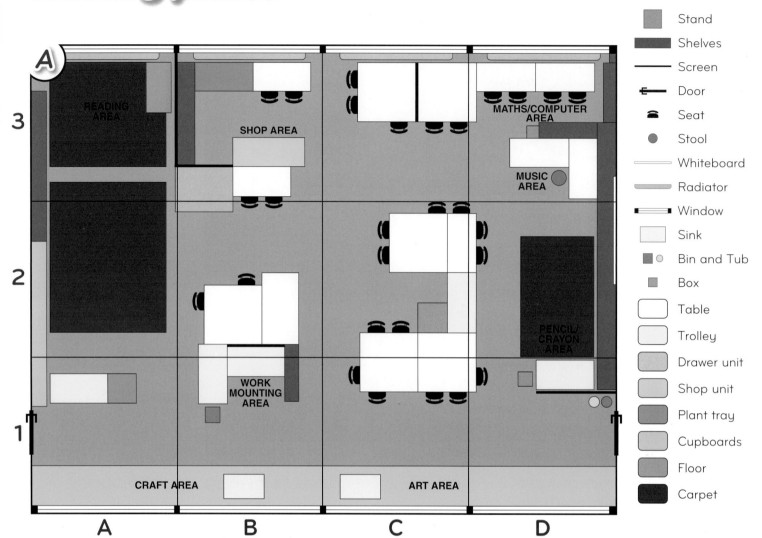

KEY

	Stand
	Shelves
	Screen
	Door
	Seat
	Stool
	Whiteboard
	Radiator
	Window
	Sink
	Bin and Tub
	Box
	Table
	Trolley
	Drawer unit
	Shop unit
	Plant tray
	Cupboards
	Floor
	Carpet

A is a plan view of a classroom. Find the shop unit. It is next to a table, not far from a window and near the middle of the room. There are lots of tables near the middle of the room, and there are eight windows in the room. It is hard to say exactly where the shop unit is.

To help you be more exact, squares have been drawn on the vertical view. These squares make a **grid**. Letters have been written along the bottom of the grid.

Numbers have been written up the side. **B** shows you how to use the letters and numbers to name a square in the grid.

To find the shop unit, put a finger on the letter **B** and a finger on the number **3**. Move your fingers up column **B** and across row **3** until they meet in the same square. This is **grid square B3**. You have found the shop unit. You can use the grid squares to say exactly where things are.

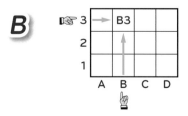

how to find a grid square

1 Using plan **A** name a feature in each of these grid squares:

   D3   A1   C2

2 Using plan **A** name a grid square which contains one of these:

   carpet   *sink*   *bin*

26

KEY

Cloak-room	Kitchen	Headteacher's room	Boiler room
← Door			
Dining area	Staffroom	Secretary's room	Corridor

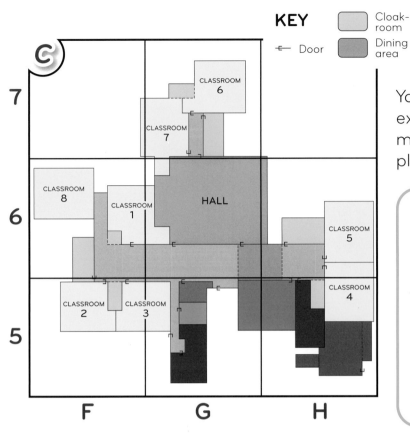

You can use grid squares to help you say exactly where features are on plans and maps. Grids have been drawn on these plans of St. Alban's School.

1 Using plan **C** name a room in each grid square: G7   H6   F5

2 Using **C** name grid squares for these features:

   Classroom 1   *Boiler room*   *Hall*

3 On plan **D** name a feature in each grid square: M11   J10   K9

4 Using **D** name grid squares for:

   Pre-school   *Shops*   *Monkswick Road*

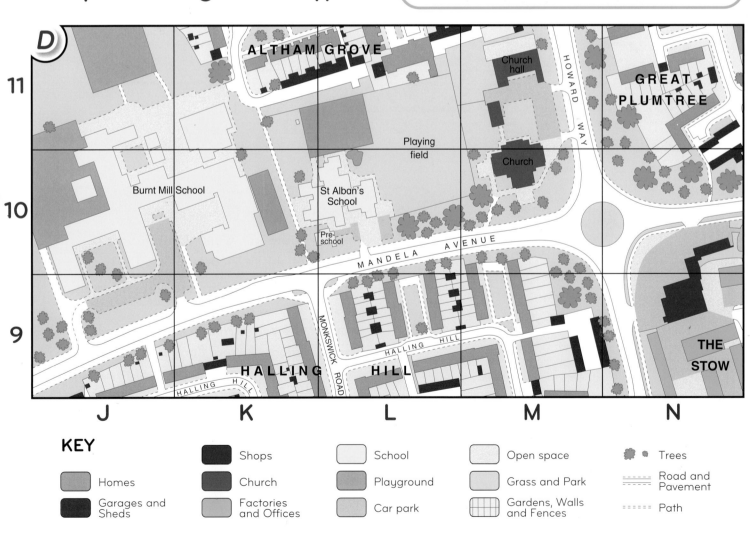

KEY

Homes	Shops
Garages and Sheds	Church
	Factories and Offices

School	Open space
Playground	Grass and Park
Car park	Gardens, Walls and Fences

Trees
Road and Pavement
Path

street maps

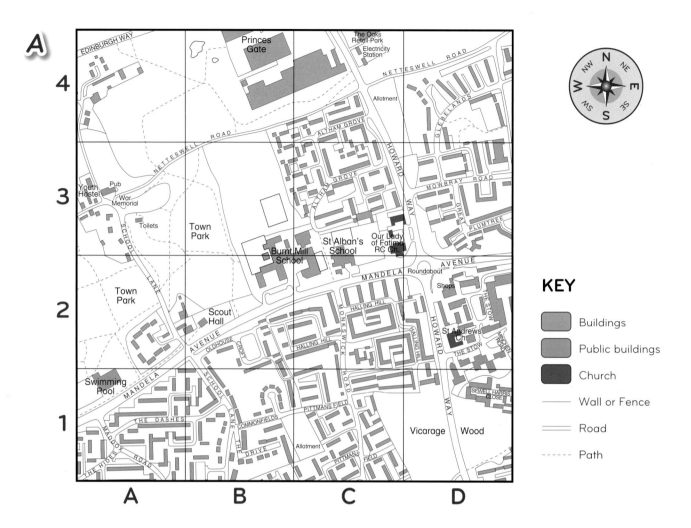

KEY

▨	Buildings
▨	Public buildings
■	Church
——	Wall or Fence
══	Road
-----	Path

A is a **street map** of the local area around St. Alban's School, which is in grid square **C3**. The street map names all the local roads. It also names some of the buildings. It shows some other places in the local area.

Street maps are useful for finding the way around a local area. Use map **A** to find your way around.

1 In which grid square is Princes Gate?

2 Which roads would you walk along from the Swimming Pool, A1, to Vicarage Wood, D1?

3 Follow this route on the map and write down the missing directions:

> *Start at the Youth Hostel in grid square A3. Go .... along School Lane and turn .... onto Mandela Avenue, to go past the Scout Hall. Turn .... onto Howard Way to go north. At the crossroads turn .... onto Netteswell Road, going west. At the end of the road you come to a Pub.*

Name two other features you arrive at.

4 Write the directions for a route of your own.

B

Index

A Allotment **C1, C4**
   Altham Grove **C3, C4**

B Burnt Mill School **B3**

C Commonfields **B1**

E Edinburgh Way **A4**
   Electricity Station **C4**

G Glebelands **D4**
   Great Plumtree **D3**

H Halling Hill **C2, D2**
   Howard Way **C3, D2**

M Maddox Road **A1**
   Mandela Avenue **A1, C2**
   Minchen Road **D2**
   Monkswick Road **C2**
   Mowbray Road **D3**

N Netteswell Road **A3, C4**

O Oldhouse Croft **B2**
   Our Lady of Fatima RC Church **C3**

P Pittmans Field **C1**
   Princes Gate **B4**
   Pub **A3**

R Roundabout **D2**

S School Lane **A3, B1**
   Scout Hall **B2**
   Sewell Harris Close **D1**
   Shops **D2**
   St Alban's School **C3**
   St Andews Church **D2**
   Swimming Pool **A1**

T The Dashes **A1**
   The Drive **B1**
   The Hides **A1**
   The Oaks Retail Park **C4**
   The Stow **D2**
   Toilets **A3**
   Town Park **A2, A3, B2, B3**

V Vicarage Wood **D1**

W War Memorial **A3**

Y Youth Hostel **A3**

All the names on the street map **A** are listed in **B**. They are listed in **alphabetical order**. This is called an **index** to the street map. The index helps us find the places on the map.

One of the streets on the map is named Commonfields. Find Commonfields in the index. Next to it is written the grid square it is in. This is called its **grid reference**. The grid reference for Commonfields is **B1**. Look at map **A** to find it.

1   Name a street that Commonfields joins on to.

2   Use the index to help you find these streets on map **A**:
    Glebelands   *The Dashes*
    Name a street each one joins on to.

3   Find out whether these streets are north or south of St. Alban's School:
    Netteswell Road   Halling Hill

4   Make an index to name places you can visit in the area in map **A**. Include these places: *Shops* D2   *Youth Hostel* A3

how far is it?

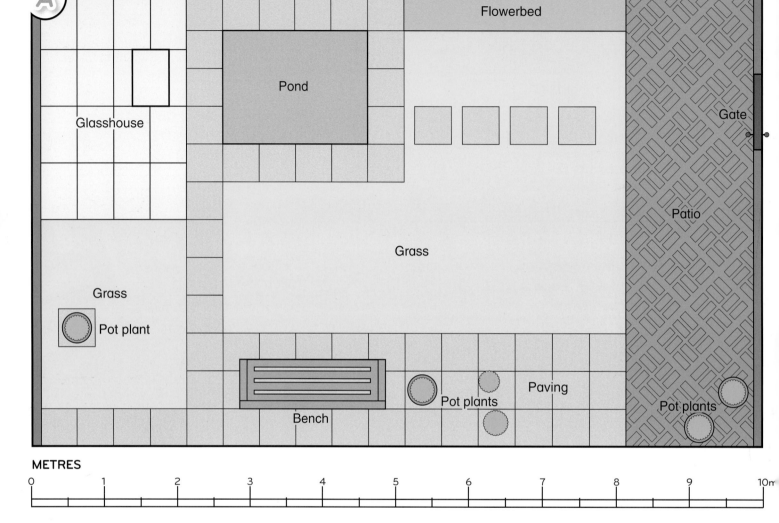

A

Flowerbed

Pond

Glasshouse

Gate

Patio

Grass

Grass

Pot plant

Bench

Pot plants

Paving

Pot plants

METRES

0   1   2   3   4   5   6   7   8   9   10m

A is a plan view of a garden. It shows the garden much smaller than it really is. But how far is it from one end of the garden to the other?

You can use the **scale bar** to find out about the real **length** of the garden. You use it to **measure** distances. **B** and **C** show you how to use the scale bar to measure how long the bench is.

Lay the edge of a piece of paper along the bench. On the paper mark the length of the bench, like **B**. Now put the paper against the scale bar so that the first mark is under the 0 on the scale. Look at the scale to see where the second mark comes, like **C**. You can see that the real length of the bench is 2 metres.

B

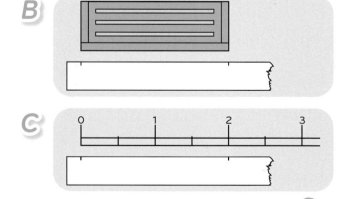

C

0   1   2   3

1   How long is the garden?

2   How wide is the garden?

3   How long is the flowerbed?

4   Which has the longest side: the glasshouse or the pond?

READING AREA

SHOP AREA

MATHS/COMPUTER AREA

MUSIC AREA

PENCIL/ CRAYON AREA

WORK MOUNTING AREA

CRAFT AREA

ART AREA

METRES

0 1 2 3 4 5 6 7 8 9 10m

D is a plan of a classroom. Use a piece of paper and the scale bar to help you measure distances and sizes in the classroom.

1 How long and wide is the classroom?

2 How long and wide are the narrow tables in the classroom?

3 How long and wide are the three carpets?

4 How far is it in a straight line from the left hand sink to the stool in the Music Area?

KEY

Stand	Sink	Whiteboard
Shelves	Seat	Radiator
Screen	Stool	Window
Door	Box	Bin and Tub

Table	Shop unit	Floor
Trolley	Plant tray	Carpet
Drawer unit	Cupboards	

31

measuring on plans and maps

You can use a ruler to measure distances on plans, in the same way that you used a piece of paper. **A** and **B** show you how to use the scale bar and a ruler to measure the length of the hall in plan **C**.

First, put your ruler on the plan so the **0** is at one end of the hall. Look to see how many centimetres it is to the other end of the hall. In **A**, you can see it is 4 centimetres.

To find the real length of the hall put your ruler along the scale bar, like **B**, and count along 4 centimetres. Look at the scale bar. It shows that the real length of the hall is 20 metres.

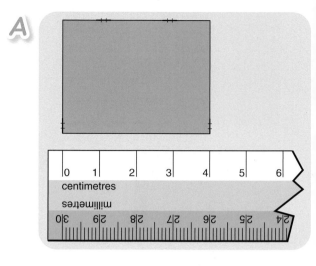

1 In a straight line, how far is it from class 5's door to class 8's door?

2 How wide are the hall and kitchen area together?

3 How long and wide is each classroom?

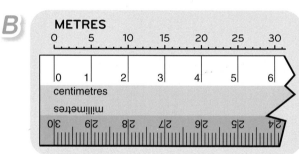

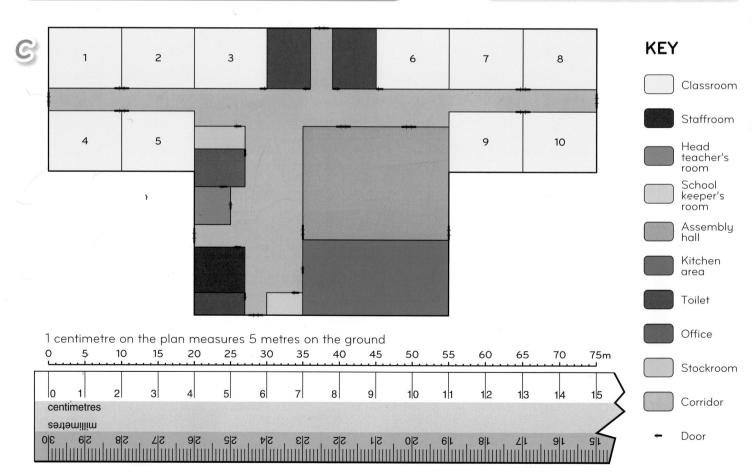

1 centimetre on the plan measures 5 metres on the ground

KEY

- ☐ Classroom
- ■ Staffroom
- ■ Head teacher's room
- ☐ School keeper's room
- ■ Assembly hall
- ■ Kitchen area
- ■ Toilet
- ■ Office
- ☐ Stockroom
- ☐ Corridor
- ⊢ Door

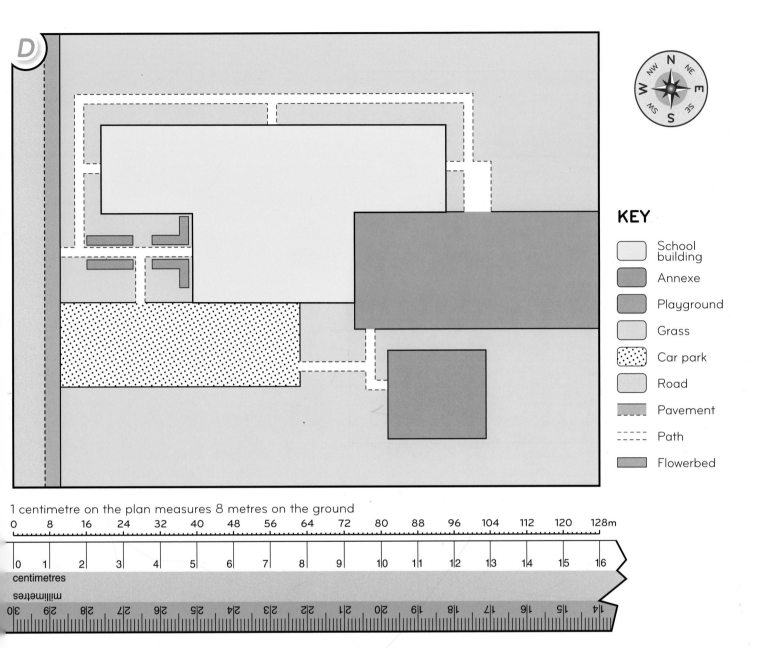

1 centimetre on the plan measures 8 metres on the ground

0   8   16   24   32   40   48   56   64   72   80   88   96   104   112   120   128m

KEY

School building

Annexe

Playground

Grass

Car park

Road

Pavement

Path

Flowerbed

When a plan or map is drawn **accurately**, like **C** and **D**, so that you can measure distances on them, we say that they have been drawn to **scale**.

Below plan **C**, you can see that the scale bar shows that 1 centimetre on the ruler measures 5 metres of the real school building. This is the scale of the plan. It is written below plan **C**.

Plan **D** shows all the school grounds. It is drawn to a smaller scale than plan **C**, so that it can be fitted onto the page. Find the scale of plan **D**.

1 How long is the school building from east to west?

2 How long and wide is the school playground?

3 How long and wide are the school grounds?

4 How far is it along the path that goes from the pavement to the door by the headteacher's room?

5 What is the scale of plan D?

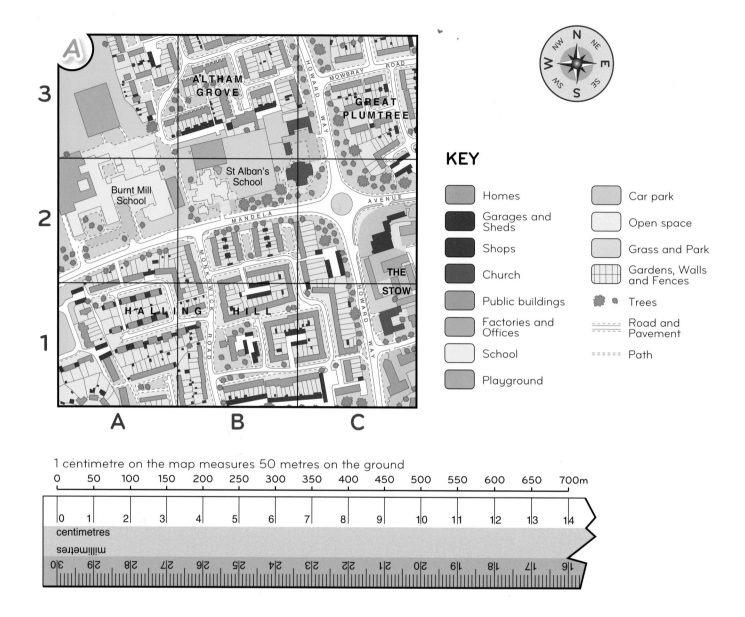

1 centimetre on the map measures 50 metres on the ground

Look at map **A** of the area around St. Alban's School. The map has been drawn to scale. All the features have been drawn accurately. You can see their shapes and sizes clearly.

Find St. Alban's School. Its grid reference is **B2**. Look at its shape. You can see all the corners of its walls.

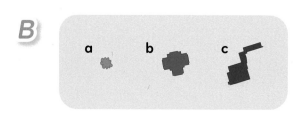

1 Find the shapes in **B** on map **A**. Name each one.

2 How far is it from the roundabout to the church in **C3** along Howard Way?

3 How long is the part of Mandela Avenue you can see across map **A**?

4 Find a grid square with six different features in it. Give its grid reference and name the features.

KEY

Homes		Car park	
Garages		Open space	
Shops		Grass and Park	
Church		Gardens	
Public buildings		Trees	
Factories and Offices		Road	
School		Path	
Playground			

1 centimetre on the map measures 100 metres on the ground

0   100   200   300   400   500   600   700   800   900   1000   1100   1200   1300   1400m

Map **C** shows more of the local area around St. Alban's School. Everything on it has been drawn smaller so that more of the local area fits onto the page. Find St. Alban's School in grid square **B2**. Its shape is roughly correct, but the map is too small to show all the corners and walls. This has happened to other features on the map too. The shapes and colours are still used to show what everything is. They are called **symbols**. The key shows what the symbols mean. You can use the scale bar to measure distances on the map.

1   Find the Scout Hall on map **C**. Draw the symbol that shows it on map **C**.

2   What is the straight line distance from the church in **C2** to the swimming pool in **A1**?

3   Why have all the trees around St. Alban's School not been drawn in? Compare the map with photo **F** on page 15.

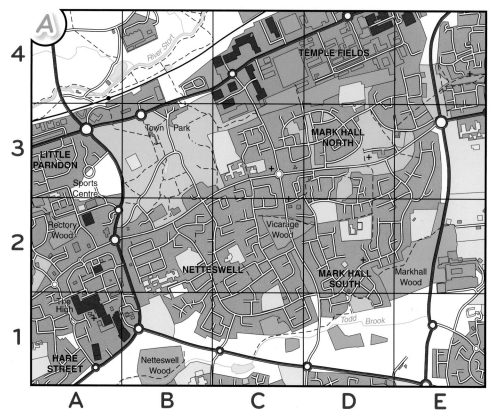

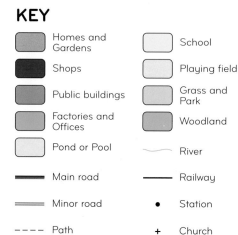

KEY

Homes and Gardens		School	
Shops		Playing field	
Public buildings		Grass and Park	
Factories and Offices		Woodland	
Pond or Pool		River	
Main road		Railway	
Minor road		• Station	
---- Path		+ Church	

1 centimetre on the map measures 250 metres on the ground

Maps **A**, **B** and **C** show more of the area around St. Alban's School. Each map shows a larger area than you have seen before.

Map **A** shows the local area of the school in the town of Harlow. The school is in grid square **C3**. On this map you can see the roads. But the homes and gardens are now shown only by a colour, not as buildings. Look in the key to see which colour symbol shows where people live.

Map **B** shows the whole of the town of Harlow. You can see that Harlow is to the west of the M11. The school is drawn so small that it is only just possible to see where it is in grid square **C3**.

On map **C** the school is not even marked. The map shows that Harlow is near other towns. Use the key to see what the symbols mean.

1 Find St. Alban's School on maps **A** and **B**. Draw the shape of the school on each map.

2 Does map **B** show more or less of the area around St. Alban's School than map **A**?

3 Look for the symbol that shows trees on each map. Do the maps show each tree or just groups of trees?

4 Find Town Park on map **A**. Draw the shape that shows where it is on maps **B** and **C**.

5 Which map tells you that the River Stort is north of Harlow?

6 Name and write the grid references of four places on map **C** which the River Stort flows past.

7 The symbols on map **C** show how the land is used, but the colour white is not shown in the key. What do you think the colour white on the map means the land is used for?

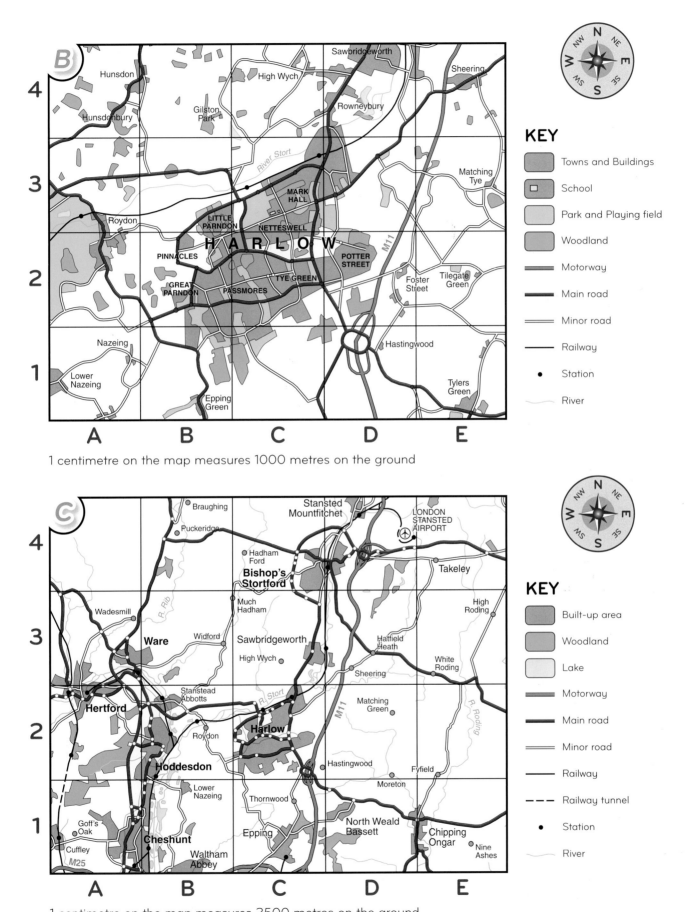

B

Hunsdon
Hunsdonbury
Gilston Park
High Wych
Sawbridgeworth
Sheering
Rowneybury
River Stort
Matching Tye
Roydon
MARK HALL
LITTLE PARNDON
NETTESWELL
H A R L O W
PINNACLES
POTTER STREET
GREAT PARNDON
TYE GREEN
PASSMORES
Foster Street
Tilegate Green
M11
Hastingwood
Nazeing
Lower Nazeing
Epping Green
Tylers Green

4
3
2
1

A   B   C   D   E

KEY

- Towns and Buildings
- School
- Park and Playing field
- Woodland
- Motorway
- Main road
- Minor road
- Railway
- Station
- River

1 centimetre on the map measures 1000 metres on the ground

C

Braughing
Puckeridge
Stansted Mountfitchet
LONDON STANSTED AIRPORT
Hadham Ford
Bishop's Stortford
Takeley
R. Rib
Wadesmill
Much Hadham
High Roding
Ware
Widford
Sawbridgeworth
Hatfield Heath
White Roding
High Wych
Sheering
R. Stort
Hertford
Stanstead Abbotts
Matching Green
R. Roding
M11
Roydon
Harlow
Hoddesdon
Hastingwood
Fyfield
Lower Nazeing
Moreton
Goff's Oak
Thornwood
Epping
North Weald Bassett
Chipping Ongar
Cheshunt
Nine Ashes
Cuffley
M25
Waltham Abbey

4
3
2
1

A   B   C   D   E

KEY

- Built-up area
- Woodland
- Lake
- Motorway
- Main road
- Minor road
- Railway
- Railway tunnel
- Station
- River

1 centimetre on the map measures 2500 metres on the ground

KEY

▨	Woodland	▬	Motorway
░	Sea and Lakes	▬	Main road
⬟ •	Towns	—	Railway
✈	Airport	∿	River

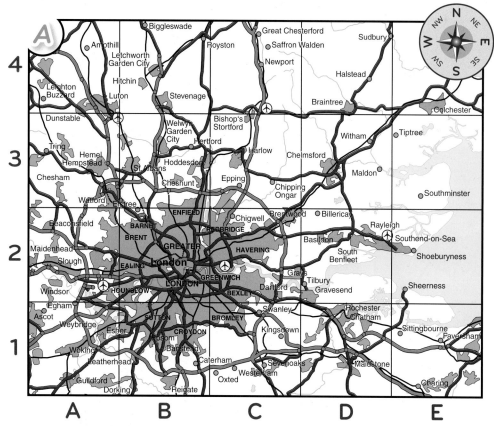

1 centimetre on the map measures 10 kilometres on the ground

Maps **A** and **B** show where Harlow is.

Map **A** shows that Harlow is north of London. It is in grid square **C3**. This map shows the large towns and main roads in the area around London.

On map **B** you can see that Harlow is in the southeast of England, in grid square **D3**. On each map more and more of England is shown. Because everything has to be drawn smaller, many features are left off the map. They are too small to show. Only the largest towns in England and Wales are shown on map **B**, but only a few are named.

KEY

░	Farmland	▨	Forest and Woodland	⬟•	Towns
▨	Moorland	░	Sea	∿	River

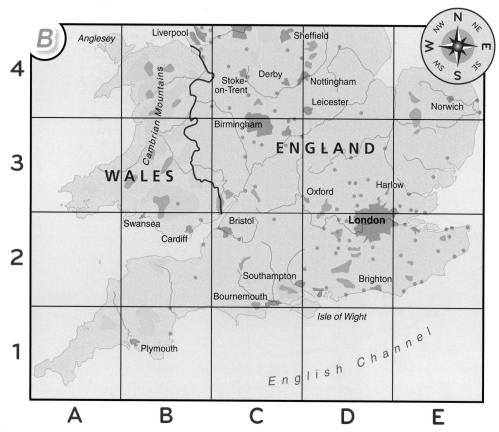

1 centimetre on the map measures 40 kilometres on the ground

1 Draw how Harlow is shown on each map.

2 Name and give the grid squares of two towns southeast of London, on map A.

3 Make an index for the towns named in England and Wales on map B.

4 Farmland is shown on map B. Which colour includes farmland on map A?

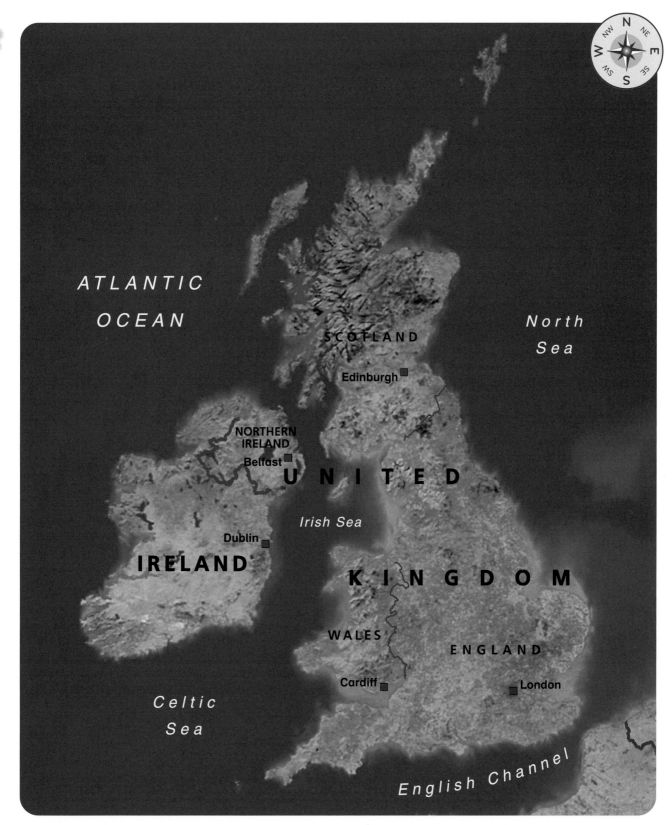

ATLANTIC
OCEAN

North
Sea

SCOTLAND

Edinburgh

NORTHERN
IRELAND
Belfast

UNITED

Irish Sea

Dublin

IRELAND

KINGDOM

WALES

ENGLAND

Cardiff

London

Celtic
Sea

English Channel

C is a satellite photo of the British Isles.
On **C** find the part of the British Isles that
you can see in map **B**.
The countries in the British Isles have been
named in the photo. The borders are
drawn in red. See what else is named.

1 Which country is north of England?

2 Which two towns are shown on **B** and **C**?

3 In which direction would you sail from
Wales to Northern Ireland?

mapping the British Isles

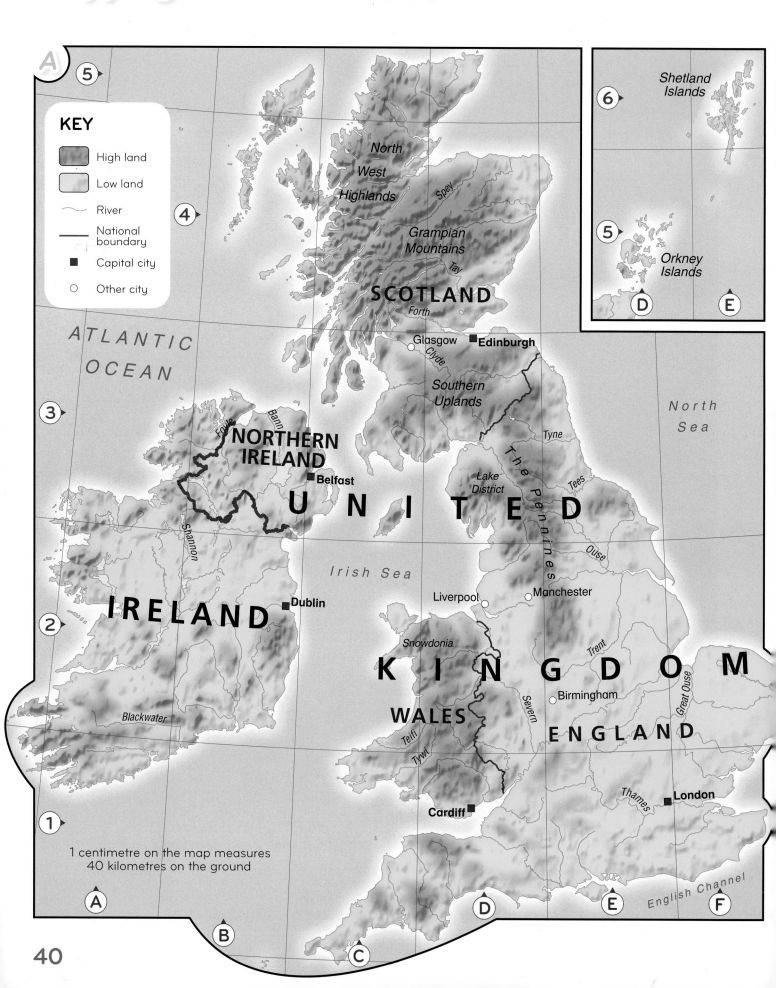

KEY

- High land
- Low land
- River
- National boundary
- ■ Capital city
- ○ Other city

A

ATLANTIC OCEAN

SCOTLAND

North West Highlands

Spey

Grampian Mountains

Tay

Forth

Glasgow ○ ■ **Edinburgh**

Clyde

Southern Uplands

NORTHERN IRELAND

Foyle

Bann

■ **Belfast**

Shannon

IRELAND

■ **Dublin**

Blackwater

U N I T E D

Lake District

The Pennines

Tyne

Tees

Ouse

North Sea

Irish Sea

Liverpool ○   ○ Manchester

K I N G D O M

Snowdonia

Teifi

Tywi

WALES

Severn

Trent

○ Birmingham

Great Ouse

E N G L A N D

Thames

■ **London**

■ **Cardiff**

1 centimetre on the map measures 40 kilometres on the ground

English Channel

Shetland Islands

Orkney Islands

40

A is a map of the British Isles. The symbols in the key tell you what the shapes, lines and colours on the map mean. Photos B to F also show you what the symbols mean.

On map A some of the rivers and areas of high land are named. The countries are named and so are their capital cities. Some other cities are named too.

1 Find Scotland on map A. Name two high land areas in Scotland.

2 Find Wales on map A. What is the name of the capital city of Wales?

3 Use maps G and A to work out which part of the United Kingdom is in the island of Ireland?

4 Name two rivers in England.

high land

low land

river

— national boundary

■ capital city

A

10 Stornoway
Lewis
Harris
North Uist
South Uist
Skye
Rum

9 Portree
Elgin
Inverness
Fraserburgh
Aberdeen
Mallaig

8 Fort William
SCOTLAND
Mull Oban
Jura
Dundee
Perth
Kirkcaldy

7 Islay
Greenock Stirling
Edinburgh
Glasgow
Kilmarnock
Arran
Campbeltown Ayr
Selkirk
Hawick
Berwick-upon-Tweed

6 Londonderry
NORTHERN IRELAND
Larne
Bangor
Belfast
Stranraer
Dumfries
Carlisle
Newcastle upon Tyne
Durham
Middlesbrough
Sligo
Workington
Darlington
Scarborough
Isle of Man
Barrow-in-Furness
Douglas

5 Westport
Drogheda
Lancaster
Blackpool
Preston
Leeds
Bradford
York
Kingston upon Hull
Galway
Athlone
Dublin
Holyhead
Anglesey
Liverpool
Manchester
Sheffield
Doncaster
Grimsby
Lincoln
Colwyn Bay
ENGLAND
IRELAND

4 Limerick
Wicklow
Chester
Stoke-on-Trent
Derby
Nottingham
Tralee
Wexford
Waterford
Stafford
Telford
Leicester
Peterborough
Norwich
Aberystwyth
Birmingham
Coventry

3 Killarney
Cork
WALES
Worcester
Hereford
Northampton
Cambridge Ipswich
Harwich
Fishguard
Merthyr Tydfil
Gloucester
Milton Keynes
Colchester
Harlow
Milford Haven
Newport
Swindon
Oxford
Southend-on-Sea
Swansea
Bristol
London
Margate
Cardiff
Bath
Reading
Canterbury
Maidstone Dover
Folkestone

2 Barnstaple
Salisbury
Taunton
Southampton
Brighton
Bournemouth
Portsmouth
Hastings
Exeter
Cowes
Weymouth
Isle of Wight
Torquay

1 Plymouth
Penzance
Isles of Scilly

A B C D E F G H

E F
Shetland Islands
12 Lerwick

Orkney Islands
11
Kirkwall

10 Wick

Map **A** shows some of the towns in each part of the British Isles.

Each town is shown by a dot, like this: •

This **symbol** shows where the town is. The name of the town is written next to it. The town of York is shown on the map like this:

•York

If we want to find where a town is on a map, we can use the **index** to help us. **B** is the index for map **A**. Find Cork in the index in **B**. The index shows it is in grid square **B3**. Find grid reference **B3** on the map.

1 Use the index in **B** to find the grid references for:
   London   Cardiff   Edinburgh   Belfast

2 Use the index to find where some other towns are on the map. Start with Stirling.

3 Is your home near or in one of the towns on the map? What is its grid reference?

4 Choose a map on another page, which has grid squares over it. Make an index for the map.

B

Index

A Aberdeen **F9**
Aberystwyth **E4**
Athlone **B5**
Ayr **D7**

B Bangor **D6**
Barnstaple **E2**
Barrow-in-Furness **E6**
Bath **F3**
Belfast **D6**
Berwick-upon-Tweed **F7**
Birmingham **F4**
Blackpool **E5**
Bournemouth **F2**
Bradford **F5**
Brighton **G2**
Bristol **F3**

C Cambridge **H3**
Campbeltown **D7**
Canterbury **H3**
Cardiff **E3**
Carlisle **E6**
Chester **F4**
Colchester **H3**
Colwyn Bay **E5**
Cork **B3**
Coventry **F4**
Cowes **G2**

D Darlington **F6**
Derby **F4**
Doncaster **G5**
Douglas **D6**
Dover **H2**

Drogheda **C5**
Dublin **C5**
Dumfries **E7**
Dundee **E8**
Durham **F6**

E Edinburgh **E8**
Elgin **E9**
Exeter **E2**

F Fishguard **D3**
Folkestone **H2**
Fort William **D8**
Fraserburgh **F9**

G Galway **A5**
Glasgow **E7**
Gloucester **F3**
Greenock **D8**
Grimsby **G5**

H Harlow **H3**
Harwich **H3**
Hastings **H2**
Hawick **F7**
Hereford **F3**
Holyhead **D5**

I Inverness **E9**
Ipswich **H3**

K Killarney **A3**
Kilmarnock **D7**
Kingston upon Hull **G5**
Kirkcaldy **E8**
Kirkwall **E11**

L Lancaster **F5**
Larne **D6**
Leeds **F5**
Leicester **G4**
Lerwick **F12**
Limerick **B4**
Lincoln **G5**
Liverpool **E5**
London **G3**
Londonderry **C7**

M Maidstone **H2**
Mallaig **D9**
Manchester **F5**
Margate **H3**
Merthyr Tydfil **E3**
Middlesbrough **G6**
Milford Haven **D3**
Milton Keynes **G3**

N Newcastle upon Tyne **F6**
Newport **E3**
Northampton **G3**
Norwich **H4**
Nottingham **G4**

O Oban **D8**
Oxford **G3**

P Penzance **D1**
Perth **E8**
Peterborough **G4**
Plymouth **E1**
Portree **D9**
Portsmouth **G2**

Preston **F5**

R Reading **G3**

S Salisbury **F2**
Scarborough **G6**
Selkirk **F7**
Sheffield **F5**
Sligo **B6**
Southampton **G2**
Southend-on-Sea **H3**
Stafford **F4**
Stirling **E8**
Stoke-on-Trent **F4**
Stornoway **C10**
Stranraer **D6**
Swansea **E3**
Swindon **F3**

T Taunton **E2**
Telford **F4**
Thurso **E10**
Torquay **E2**
Tralee **A4**

U Ullapool **D10**

W Waterford **C4**
Westport **A5**
Wexford **C4**
Weymouth **F2**
Wick **E10**
Wicklow **C4**
Worcester **F3**
Workington **E6**

Y York **G5**

Europe

A

ATLANTIC OCEAN

North Sea

Rhine

Alps

Danube

Mediterranean Sea

A is a satellite photo of part of Europe. Find the land and the sea. Some of the mountains and rivers have been named on **A**. It also shows the seas around Europe.

You can see the whole of Europe in map **B**. If you watch or listen to the news, you will often hear the names of countries in Europe.

Map **B** shows where each country is and which countries are neighbours. Some countries have many neighbours; others have few.

The colours on map **B** show the shape of each country. The red lines on the map show the borders of each country.

1 Which ocean is north of Europe?

2 Which countries have only one neighbour?

3 Which country has the most neighbours?

4 How many countries are there in Europe?

5 Name the country both France and Portugal have a border with.

6 Name the country which has Germany, Austria, Italy and France around it.

7 Find the Alps in **A**. Name a country on **B** where you could visit the Alps.

8 Which is the most eastern country in Europe?

9 Listen to the news on the radio or TV. Make a list when European countries are named. Find them on a map of Europe.

B

ARCTIC OCEAN

N NW NE W E SW SE S

③

ICELAND
■ Reykjavík

A

ATLANTIC
OCEAN

NORWAY

SWEDEN

FINLAND

RUSSIAN

E

Oslo
Stockholm

Helsinki
St Petersburg

FEDERATION

Tallinn
ESTONIA

Moscow

Edinburgh *North*
Belfast *Sea*
UNITED
Dublin
IRELAND KINGDOM

DENMARK
Copenhagen

LATVIA
Rīga

LITHUANIA
Vilnius
8

Minsk

②

Amsterdam
The
Hague **7**
London

Berlin

BELARUS

Kiev

1 BELGIUM
2 BOSNIA-HERZEGOVINA
3 KOSOVO
4 LIECHTENSTEIN
5 LUXEMBOURG
6 MONTENEGRO
7 NETHERLANDS
8 RUSSIAN FEDERATION
9 SLOVENIA
10 SWITZERLAND

Brussels **1**
5

GERMANY

Warsaw
POLAND

UKRAINE

Paris

Prague
CZECH REPUBLIC

SLOVAKIA

MOLDOVA
Chişinău

Munich

Vienna
Bratislava

FRANCE

Bern **4**
10

AUSTRIA
9
Ljubljana
Milan

Budapest
HUNGARY

Odesa

Lyon

SAN
MARINO

Zagreb
CROATIA

Belgrade
SERBIA

ROMANIA
Bucharest

Black Sea

MONACO

Sarajevo
2

BULGARIA
Sofia

ANDORRA

ITALY

6 **3**
Skopje
Tirana MACEDONIA
ALBANIA

PORTUGAL

Madrid

Barcelona

TURKEY

Istanbul

Lisbon

SPAIN

Rome

ASIA

①

Gibraltar *(UK)*

GREECE
Athens

Mediterranean Sea

B

AFRICA

C

MALTA

D

KEY ◢ Countries — Country boundary ■ Capital city ○ Other important city

1 centimetre on the map measures 200 kilometres on the ground

45

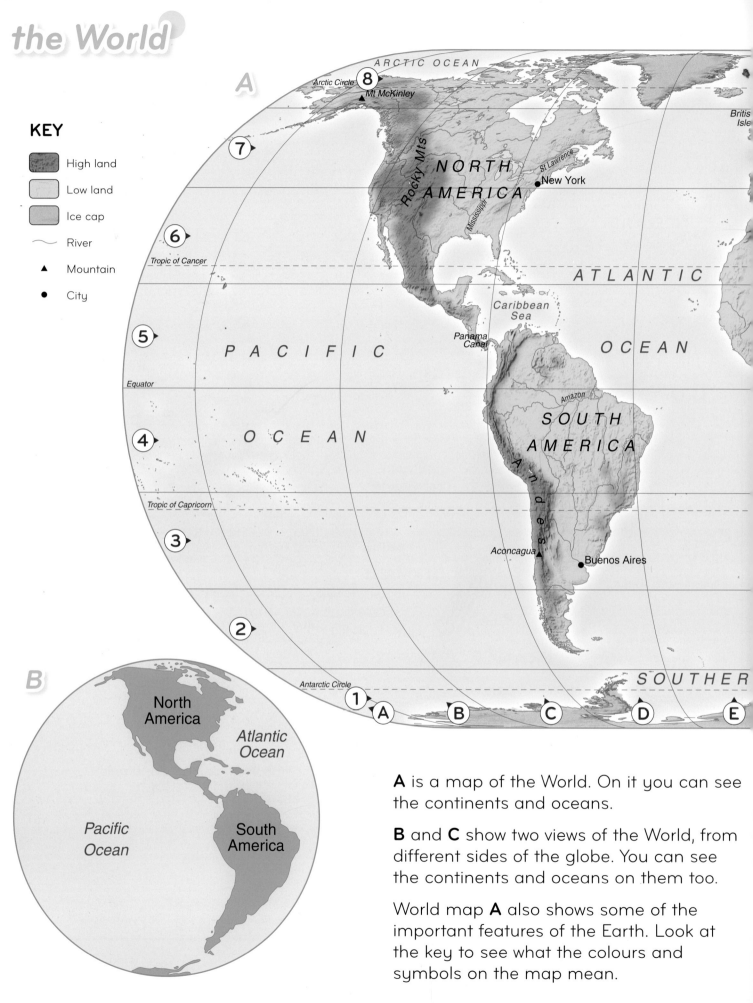

KEY

■	High land
▢	Low land
▨	Ice cap
∿	River
▲	Mountain
●	City

ARCTIC OCEAN

Arctic Circle ⑧

▲ Mt McKinley

A

⑦

NORTH AMERICA

Rocky Mts

St Lawrence

● New York

Britis Isle

⑥

Tropic of Cancer

ATLANTIC

⑤

PACIFIC

Caribbean Sea

Panama Canal

OCEAN

Equator

④

OCEAN

Amazon

SOUTH AMERICA

Andes

Tropic of Capricorn

③

Aconcagua ▲

● Buenos Aires

②

SOUTHER

Antarctic Circle

① Ⓐ   Ⓑ   Ⓒ   Ⓓ   Ⓔ

B

North America

Atlantic Ocean

Pacific Ocean

South America

A is a map of the World. On it you can see the continents and oceans.

B and **C** show two views of the World, from different sides of the globe. You can see the continents and oceans on them too.

World map **A** also shows some of the important features of the Earth. Look at the key to see what the colours and symbols on the map mean.

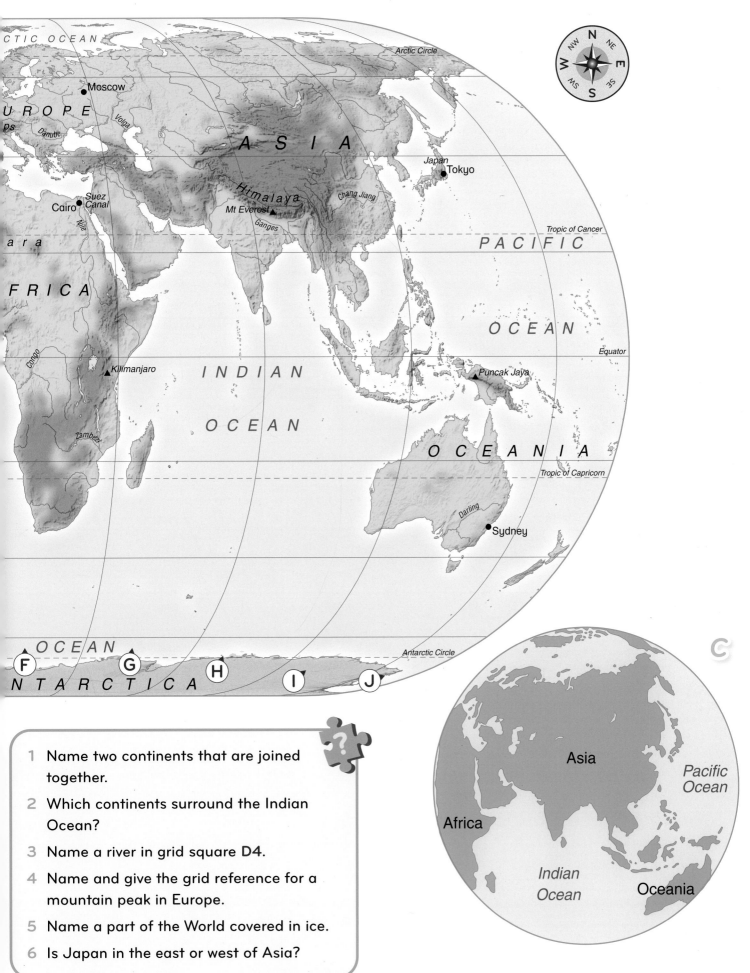

CTIC OCEAN

Arctic Circle

• Moscow

U R O P E

ps

Danube

Volga

A S I A

Japan
• Tokyo

Suez
Canal

Cairo •

Himalaya

Chang Jiang

Mt Everest ▲

Tropic of Cancer

Nile

Ganges

P A C I F I C

a r a

F R I C A

Congo

▲ Kilimanjaro

I N D I A N

O C E A N

Equator

▲ Puncak Jaya

Zambezi

O C E A N

O C E A N I A

Tropic of Capricorn

Darling

• Sydney

O C E A N

Antarctic Circle

Ⓕ   Ⓖ   Ⓗ   Ⓘ   Ⓙ

N T A R C T I C A

1 Name two continents that are joined together.

2 Which continents surround the Indian Ocean?

3 Name a river in grid square D4.

4 Name and give the grid reference for a mountain peak in Europe.

5 Name a part of the World covered in ice.

6 Is Japan in the east or west of Asia?

Asia

Pacific Ocean

Africa

Indian Ocean

Oceania

teacher's notes

ideas/skills	resources	extension activities

looking at plans and maps: perspective, symbols and key

	ideas/skills	resources	extension activities
2-3	Drawing round object bases to make a plan. • the view from above: plan and shape • identifying objects in plan view • vocabulary: shape, plan	• objects to look obliquely and straight down on • vertical photos of objects • plans of objects for children to identify • toys, overhead projector (OHP)	• draw plans of objects for others to identify • match plans to pictures of objects: elevation, oblique, vertical • project base-shape of toy onto screen by placing toy on OHP, draw round toy, remove toy, leave plan
4-5	Identifying features on vertical aerial photos and matching them to a map. Interpreting symbols using maps. • terms 'oblique view' and 'vertical view' • matching oblique and vertical views	• school area oblique and vertical photos and large scale map e.g. 1:1250 or 1:2500 scale • aerial photos and large scale maps of other localities	• discuss what can be seen in the photos • find features on oblique and vertical aerial photos • look at how features are shown on the local map • compare the map symbols to the feature shapes on the vertical aerial photo
6-7	Identifying British Isles, Europe and continents on maps and globes. • satellite and space photos • identifying shapes of areas on photos and maps	• satellite/space photos of Earth • inflatable globes and globe on stand • maps of continents and Earth • cut-out shapes of continents and other large areas of the Earth, e.g. islands	• match satellite photos of continents with shapes of the continents on map/globe • pass inflatable globe round the class/group, call out the name of a continent/ocean/island, child to find, then pass on
8-9	Interpreting symbols using maps. Identifying features from vertical viewpoints and matching them to a map. • plan as showing layout and shape of features and names	• photos of part of classroom • plans of room: accurate/with errors • cue cards for: location, direction, size and distance	• children to draw own plan of room • give children plan of room which includes errors, for children to identify and correct • use cue cards for finding features in, and routes around, the room and plans of it • use features and plan to orient plan correctly
10-11	Interpreting symbols using maps. Following routes and describing the location of features using maps. • relating oblique and aerial photos • using colour code for categories of use	• oblique/vertical photos of school • plans of school building • base maps of the rooms in school • simple verbal (taped/written) directions to follow routes around school	• discuss where rooms are in school and how to get to them • make a survey of room use in school; make a colour coded school use map; create a key • give directions for drawing routes on a base map
12-13	Identifying features on vertical aerial photos and matching them to a map. Interpreting symbols and describing the location of places using maps. • showing larger area in same space	• photos of school and grounds from a variety of angles • map of school and grounds • copy of large scale OS map of the school: 1:1250 or 1:2500 scale	• find where ground level photos were taken, match in situ and on map; mark where taken on map • mark routes on a map of the school grounds • use a base map of the school grounds, survey the use of land, colour code and create key
14-15	Identifying features on vertical aerial photos and matching them to a map. Interpreting symbols, following routes and locating places using maps. • when more of an area is shown, everything is drawn smaller	• photos of features in local area • oblique and vertical aerial photos • OS maps of the local area: 1:1250 or 1:2500 scale and 1:10 000 scale • photos of local road signs and road names • plan shapes of individual features	• match oblique and vertical photos and ground level photos with local area maps • locate street signs on local map, using sign and background information in photo; go out to find some near school • find shapes on photos and map, identify features

varieties of maps

	ideas/skills	resources	extension activities
16-17	Making maps of routes. Making sketch maps of small areas showing the main features and using symbols with a key. • drawing a map for a purpose, map/selective	• photos of features around local area • vertical photo and large scale OS and street maps of local area • teacher drawn maps of different parts of local area	• children to draw maps of home/school area showing sites of local facilities and features, e.g. park, shops, garage, etc • check accuracy of map against OS/street maps • give children photos of known local landmarks and ask them to draw map to show you where they are and how to get there
18-19	Extracting information from pictorial maps. Using pictures to identify features and find out about places. • use of familiar story for mapwork	• copy of Fantastic Mr. Fox (Roald Dahl) • other stories in which there are pictures/maps of human and physical landscapes/environments	• Read Fantastic Mr. Fox and encourage use of the map during the story • encourage children to make their own maps of the areas in which they set their stories • read other stories using or creating maps of the places set in
20-21	Using maps as sources of information. • develops idea of a variety of maps • ways information can be shown on maps • maps for particular purposes	• copies of a variety of maps, e.g. from adverts, postcards, newspapers, tourist brochures, magazines, websites • photos of maps seen in the local area	• discuss what maps show, who might use them, usefulness, if they could be better drawn; discuss why these maps are provided • make keys for maps without keys • compare maps of different types of the local area

finding places: direction and location

	ideas/skills	resources	extension activities
22-23	Using the eight points of the compass. Interpreting symbols using a map. Identifying land and sea on maps. • vocabulary: north, east, south, west	• transparent compass rose showing north, east, south, west as an overlay • compasses, large for demonstration and small for personal use	• use compass to find direction N, E, S and W in classroom and playground (explore effect of iron) and mark on classroom/school walls • use overlay on playground/treasure island maps • discuss the usefulness of compass directions • link to types of maps provided with stories, re key, compass
24-25	Using the eight points of the compass. Interpreting symbols and following routes using maps.	• direction compasses for individual use • plans and maps of school and local area with compass rose on	• follow/give directions walking round classroom and school using compass and giving compass directions • find out about how a compass works and what can disrupt it